THE
STREETS OF
OLD NEW YORK

A Pictorial Rebirth

of a Vanished City

THE
STREETS OF
OLD NEW YORK

BY

J. ERNEST BRIERLY

HASTINGS HOUSE, PUBLISHERS

NEW YORK

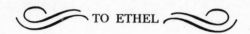 TO ETHEL

PREFACE

When reading about some especially interesting historical event, it is not unnatural to wish to see the place where it occurred and also just how the place looked in the distant past.

A student of European or Asiatic history can still do this, in spite of the great destruction wrought by countless wars. Even now, one can walk through the old palaces and churches, many of which have survived and are still, to a great extent, just as they were when the great men and women of history lived and acted in them.

In this way, the student can increase the knowledge and pleasure derived from reading, by actual seeing.

However, a student of New York City's history, who hopes to follow this method of study, will find his or her hopes frustrated for, of all the many historic buildings, numbers of them fine examples of the architecture of the time, dating from the Dutch founding in 1626 and continuing through the British Colonial period up to the American Revolution in 1776, only three are standing today on the entire island of Manhattan.

Since New York has outdistanced all the other cities of the world in so many ways, it seems a pity that she should be at the foot of the class, when it comes to historic buildings. In spite of all this, one encouraging fact remains: the streets of the old city, many bearing their old names, are still with us.

With these old streets as a basis, and by careful study and research among old maps, prints and books on architecture, costume, implements and vehicles, it has been possible in a fashion, to rebuild the vanished old houses and repopulate them with some of the people, appearing as they did in the days of long ago.

The following pages will show these reconstructed Streets of Old New York.

J. Ernest Brierly

THE
STREETS OF
OLD NEW YORK

BROAD STREET

As you hurry along Broad Street, pushing your way through the crowds and dodging the taxis, it is interesting, if you can spare the time, to picture the same street as it appeared about three centuries ago. At this time, 1637, it was called the "Heere Graft" and was one of the first four streets of the town, then called New Amsterdam. A canal ran down its centre, beginning at a swamp where cattle grazed (now Exchange Place) and running south to the bay, below, where tall-masted Dutch ships rode at anchor. Merchandise was transported from these ships, by small boats, to the warehouses and quaint Dutch dwellings which lined the shores of the canal. Two bridges spanned the canal at intervals and here the Dutch burghers congregated to gossip and discuss business.

In 1638, Dominie Everardus Bogardus and his attractive wife, the Widow Annetje Jans, occupied this house with the famous silver knocker. Earlier, in 1633, the Dominie had brought about the erection of the first church edifice in the town and had been its pastor. Following his marriage, he came into control of the widow's valuable sixty-two-acre farm, adjoining the Company's Bouwerie, which added to his prestige. He had also been partly responsible for Governor Kieft's appointment and, in 1642, at the wedding feast of his step-daughter, had helped to engineer the collection of moneys for the building of a second and finer church, "the Church in the Fort". Thus, the Dominie did his part in making the history of Old New York.

Peter Koch (or Kocks) appears to have been the first house owner at No. 1 Broadway. He is said to have been a sergeant in the initial military force sent over from Holland, to serve under Wouter Van Twiller, in 1633. Some time after his arrival, he built and operated a tavern at the present No. 1 Broadway, patronized mainly by soldiers from the fort. After William Kieft became Director General, in 1638, Koch accompanied Dr. La Montagne on expeditions against the Indians. By telling of his adventures, upon returning from these expeditions, he added considerably to the popularity of his tavern. He is also credited with having concocted the first Martini cocktail ever to be served in this country.

In 1644, near the junction of the present Pearl and Whitehall Streets, Tryntje Jonas had her little house, just behind the home of her famous daughter, Annetje Jans Bogardus. Tryntje was one of the first medical women to practice her profession in Manhattan for which she received a small salary from the Dutch West India Company. Occasionally, a barber-surgeon came ashore from an anchored ship, but the first doctor to make history in Manhattan was Jacob Hendricksen Varrenvanger, about 1649. This doctor showed real sympathy and understanding in his care for the sick and, in 1658, founded probably the first hospital in North America. This was the forerunner of Bellevue Hospital of today.

BATTERY PLACE

In 1660, this windmill held the distinction in the city which today is held by New York's skyscrapers. It towered above most of the neighboring buildings. The lookout on an incoming ship scanned the horizon for this landmark and steered accordingly. The mill stood on rising ground just west of the fort, where it could catch the wind from all directions. It was an important adjunct to the business of the town. The monopoly of bolting flour was instrumental in making New York a great seaport. Until 1684, the law stated that no bread or flour could be exported from the Province, except through the port of New York (New Amsterdam). The windmill has gone but its memory still survives on the Seal of the City. Its four sails quarter the shield diagonally, leaving spaces for two flour barrels and two beavers; these latter are symbols of the old Dutch fur trade.

BRIERLY

In the old Dutch days, our present Wall Street was an open way, running along a high stockade of wooden palisades, and was known as the "Cingle". The stockade was the result of a rumor, in 1653, that the New Englanders were planning a foray upon the town. The only defense against invasion was the small fort at the south end of the island, not large enough to hold all the townsfolk and their belongings, so the frightened Dutch got busy and built a palisade or "wall" about ten feet high with a bank of earth on the inside to strengthen it, from which the defenders could look down upon any possible attackers. There was a fortified "Water Gate" at the East River end and a "Land Gate" where the present Broadway crosses Wall Street. Through this land gate, the burghers with their cattle and produce had intercourse with the open country to the northward. Incidentally, the attack on the wall never materialized.

BRIERLY

In 1660, this stone bridge spanning the canal where, today, Stone Street reaches Broad, was a busy spot. From the fort, at Bowling Green one walked through Stone Street and, crossing this bridge, continued along Pearl Street (then called Perel Straat), which skirted the East River; then, through the "Water Gate" in the stockade at Wall Street and eventually reached the ferry landing (now Peck's Slip), from which he could cross the East River to Breukelen (Brooklyn). Besides being a segment of an important traffic artery, this bridge was the meeting place of burghers, who discussed business deals involving sizable sums of money. Oddly enough, just a few blocks north of this bridge, today, we have the New York Stock Exchange, where business still continues to be transacted, though on a somewhat larger scale than in the old Dutch days.

1635

BRIERLY

The nearest approach to a church service by the first Dutch settlers was the occasional reading of the Scriptures by two laymen, who had come over with Peter Minuit. They were called "Krankbesoeckers" or "comforters of the sick". The first regular church services were conducted by Dominie Jonas Michaelius in the vacant loft of a horse mill. Dominie Michaelius was succeeded by Dominie Everardus Bogardus, a forceful man, who refused to preach in a loft, and the result was a rough wooden church, the first on the island, at the present Pearl Street near Broad, 1633. Later, David De Vries, a distinguished citizen and soldier, returning from a visit to New England, told of the fine churches he had seen there and, through his influence, the second Dutch Church was erected in 1642. It was a large stone structure, built in the fort, and was called the Church of St. Nicholas.

PECK SLIP AT PEARL STREET

In 1664 or thereabouts, anyone wishing to be ferried across the East River to Brooklyn could blow a blast on a long metal horn, suspended from a tree, growing close to the water's edge (today, Peck Slip at Pearl Street). Upon hearing this blast, Harmanus van Borsum, the ferryman, would gladly leave his work in a nearby field, answer the call, unfasten his boat, moored to the aforesaid tree and, for about six cents each, row the waiting customers across the river to "Breukelen". But, if a high wind were blowing, high enough to cause the sails of the windmill near the fort to be taken in, the customers would be obliged to wait until the weather changed.

BRIERLY

In 1664, the last year of Peter Stuyvesant's governorship of New Amsterdam, before the British occupation, the "Water Gate" at the intersection of the present Wall and Pearl Streets, was the most important point of entry in the barricade which guarded the northern boundary of the town. Every night, at eight o'clock, the watchmen were called out and, at nine o'clock, a bell was rung as a signal to close all the city gates. At ten o'clock, every tavern was closed and no more customers were admitted. Any customers already in a tavern at this hour were not allowed to leave, but had to stay there until the signal for the opening of the city gates the following morning at day break. "Freedom of Choice", as we know it today, did not exist.

BRIERLY

In 1664, the Articles of Capitulation, delivering New Amsterdam to the British, were signed in this house. The conquered Dutch citizens were guaranteed security of their property, customs, conscience and religion. This tolerant treatment enabled ex-Governor Stuyvesant, after reporting to his superiors in Holland, to return to his beloved farm and spend there perhaps the happiest years of his life, free from political cares and surrounded by his well-kept orchards and flower gardens. He died here in 1672. He was a man of strong character and, after almost three hundred years, Stuyvesant's is the best remembered name in the history of New Amsterdam. Even from a material viewpoint, Stuyvesant is outstanding for, although nearly every other material evidence of the old town, its houses and its citizens has disappeared forever, Stuyvesant's bones have survived the march of time and today rest peacefully in a vault in St. Mark's-in-the-Bouwerie, in the midst of his erstwhile country estate.

BRIERLY

Unknown to most New Yorkers, a mill stream once flowed from the present Central Park, in a winding south-easterly direction, to the East River. It flowed through the sixty-acre farm which Governor Sir Edmund Andros, appointee of the Duke of York, had granted to David Duffore in 1677. The following year, 1678, the Bolting Act became law. This act gave New York City the sole and exclusive right to grind and export flour. Duffore, taking advantage of this golden opportunity, built a grist mill on his stream and operated it successfully. This stream, called Devoor's Mill Stream, no longer flows through sunlit glades and fertile meadows, but now continues its course, unseen, far beneath the pavement, finally reaching the East River near 49th Street.

LOWER PEARL STREET

Jacob Leisler, a well-intentioned German, by hard work and honest dealings had gained wealth, a deaconship in the church and the love and trust of the ordinary people; but lack of tact had produced enemies among the more influential. In 1689, Lieut. Governor Nicholson (suspected of conspiring to restore James II to power, aided by Louis XIV and Frontenac) was forced to leave New York. Leisler, following a noisy demonstration before his house in the Strand (lower Pearl Street) was made commander of the fort and custom house by a "Committee of Safety" until they should receive orders from King William. When the King's governor, Sloughter, arrived he sent an officer, verbally demanding Leisler's surrender. Leisler refused to do so without a written order from the King. This resulted in Leisler's arrest. He was convicted of murder and treason and hanged. In 1698, Parliament annulled these charges, thus saving his honor but not his life.

PEARL STREET

In 1695, Col. Abraham De Peyster built his palatial mansion on Queen Street (Pearl St.). Some of its rooms were forty feet deep, with handsomely decorated walls and ceilings and were furnished with costly imported furniture and paintings by the Old Masters. The grounds occupied an entire city block and the front balcony for almost a century was the favorite resort for governors when reviewing passing parades. Col. De Peyster was descended from a Huguenot family belonging to the French nobility who, in 1572, had fled to Holland to escape the Massacre of Saint Bartholomew. About 1650, Johannes De Peyster, who was founder of the family in New York, came here with considerable capital, increased it by investments, mainly in shipping, and held important positions in the church and government, under both the Dutch and British. Governer Nicholls said De Peyster could make a better platform speech than any man outside of Parliament.

De Peyster Arms

BRIERLY

PEARL STREET

Pearl Street, until recently, darkened by the elevated structure and lined by shabby old buildings, once ran along the water's edge and was probably the most important street in the town. It certainly is one of the four oldest. When the Dutch built Fort Amsterdam in 1626, a road including Stone and Pearl Streets was laid out, connecting the fort, at what is now Bowling Green, with the present Peck Slip, where a ferry ran across the East River to Long Island. After the British took the city in 1664, and re-named it New York, this road (Pearl Street) was called Queen Street and on it, at its junction with Maiden Lane, Roger Baker established the first English inn in the city. It was named the King's Head and had a sign hanging over the door upon which was painted a portrait of King William of Orange. Not only travelers and sea-rovers congregated here but also highly respectable members of the Committees of Council and Assembly to discuss affairs of state. In those days the inn was an important part of the community.

New York's second French Protestant "Eglise du St. Esprit" was erected in 1704, on King Street (now Pine). Long before this, many Walloon and Huguenot families had found refuge in New York and the French were gaining prestige in the town. Peter Minuit was a Huguenot and Rev. Jonas Michaelius, in 1628, gave the first administration of the Lord's Supper to fifty Walloon communicants. As the French population increased, church services were held in various places under varying conditions. By 1687, there were about two hundred French families in the town, including the Cregiers, de la Montagnes, Bayards, Savarians, de Silles, Jays and de Lancys and, in 1688, the "Eglise française a la Nouvelle York", the first church devoted exclusively to French services, was erected in Pettycoat Lane (later Marketfield Street). The site was later covered by the Produce Exchange.

BRIERLY

BROADWAY AND RECTOR STREET

By wandering around the old tombstones in Trinity Churchyard today and studying the names and inscriptions on them, it is quite possible to bring back to life a picture of old New York, following the Stuyvesant period. Many of the men and women who lie buried here played a prominent part in the city's history. The first "Trinity" was built in 1697 on the site occupied by the present or third structure. Colonel Benjamin Fletcher, then governor, had a special pew built in the church for his own use. The first rector was the Reverend William Vesey. A large tract of land, known as the Queen's Farm, was included in the grant to the corporation, thus making Trinity the wealthiest parish in America. The wise use of this ever-increasing wealth has enabled the church to help the city in many ways in its progress through the years. The original church was destroyed by the fire of 1776.

BRIERLY

When George Washington was born in 1732, this region was farm country. A creek, which the Dutch called Minnetta Water, crossed it toward the southwest. To the west was Bossen Bouwerie (later Greenwich Village) and, to the east, Bouwerie Lane, Peter Stuyvesant's mansion and its adjoining Dutch hamlet. The remainder of the surrounding country was farm land with an occasional manor house. Gradually this section became urbanized, following the "Commissioners' Plan" (1807-1811). Fifth Avenue was opened in 1837 and, some years previously, the old Potters' Field had been transformed into aristocratic Washington Square, which was soon bordered by fine residences. Years passed and the Washington Arch was erected. Since 1732, a great transformation had taken place. Even Washington's Birthday had changed. In the Family Bible, the date of George's birth was February eleventh. This was because England didn't accept the Gregorian revision of the calendar until 1752. This acceptance made it necessary to push the Old Style dates ahead, and February eleventh became February twenty-second.

In 1730, Anthony Rutgers, a respected member of a distinguished family, built a "prodigiously fine dwelling" near the corner of Thomas Street and Broadway. This was well out of town and Broadway ended some distance south of the hill upon which the house stood, owing to the fact that an inaccessible swamp extended across the island from Collect Pond to the Hudson. Rutgers proposed that the King's Council grant him this swampland on condition that he drain it within a year. Since the land was useless and a breeder of disease, Rutgers' request was granted. He transformed it into rich farm land, thus enriching himself and also improving the health of the community. After his death, in 1750, this land was called Lispenard's Meadow, Rutgers' married daughter's name. His residence and garden were leased to John Jones, who ran it as a place of entertainment, called "Ranelagh". After 1773, it was replaced by the New York Hospital.

BRIERLY

Although the coffee berry was sold in New York as early as 1683, we hear no mention of a coffee house until 1705. But in 1743, the Merchants' Coffee House appeared upon the scene, at the corner of Wall and Water Streets, then the shore line region known as Coffee House Slip. Here gathered all business and shipping interests of the city (as at Lloyd's in London). Until it was burned in 1804, this coffee house entertained such organizations as the N. Y. Hospital, Chamber of Commerce and the Society of Cincinnati. In addition to these, a group of gentlemen who had organized the New York Stock Exchange in May, 1792, at a table under a tree fronting No. 60 Wall Street, decided to make this old coffee house their headquarters. These gentlemen had been known as the traders "under the Buttonwood Tree".

GREENWICH STREET

Greenwich Street is one of New York's old-timers. Although, in 1633, Wouter van Twiller, the Dutch Governor, owned a farm which included much of the present Greenwich Village, there was apparently no good road connecting it with lower Manhattan until the British occupation, so Van Twiller must have traveled back and forth by boat. In 1746, Captain Peter Warren of his Majesty's frigate Launceston, built himself a fine residence near the present Sheridan Square, and, from this time on, we hear much of the Greenwich Road leading from this location to the city. This old road followed the same course as Greenwich Street of today, starting at the Battery and ending at Greenwich Village. It ran along the shore of the Hudson River. All of the present-day streets between it and the river have been added at various periods, by filling in the river and thus extending the city's area. When at home, after one of his many voyages, Captain Warren, later Sir Peter, could relax on the veranda of his splendid mansion and see his good ship, the Launceston, anchored off shore in the Hudson.

BRIERLY

In 1750, the Blue Bell Tavern stood on the corner of the present 181st Street and Broadway, which was then the Kingsbridge Road, even then a very important thoroughfare. This was nine miles north of the city, so travelers reaching the tavern late in the afternoon, usually spent the night here. During the Revolution, the country hereabout was the scene of much fighting. Fort Washington was only a short distance away, to the northward. In 1776, after a fierce engagement in which the Patriots rolled huge rocks down the hill upon the advancing Hessians, they were at last forced to surrender and the British forces took possession of the fort.

This tavern was originally the mansion of the Honorable James De Lancey, Lieutenant Governor of the Province. It was built in 1700 by Etienne de Lancey, founder of the family in this country. The mansion was of stone, two stories high, with a cupola and, from the back piazza, across a sloping lawn, one had an unobstructed view of the Hudson River and the Palisades. Opened as a tavern in 1754, by Edward Willett, it became the outstanding hostelry of the town. It had fine adjoining stables and was handy to the Boston Post Road and the North River and Brooklyn Ferries. Its proximity to the fashionable "Church Walk" added to its distinction. In 1774, John Adams stopped here, on his way to Philadelphia, where the seeds of the American Revolution would take root.

BRIERLY

BROADWAY AT LEONARD STREET

Until the opening of the Greenwich Road, at an uncertain date prior to 1760, Broadway, as a thoroughfare, ended at the present Leonard Street. It was cut off here by a set of bars, through which cattle were led to graze in the pastures to the northward. This side of the town had been by-passed, as the east side was considered much more desirable for dwelling and also for business. All the docks were on the East River for, being salt water, it didn't freeze and was safe for shipping the year round. The east side was also accessible to the Brooklyn Ferry and to the north, while the west side was cut off by swampland. It was not until this swampland was drained that Broadway got its real chance to eventually become what some enthusiasts have called "The Greatest Street in the World".

BRIERLY

The first Hoppers (Hoppe) came to New York from Holland in 1652. In 1714, Matthys Adolphus Hoppe owned a large farm stretching along the Hudson, northward from about 42nd Street and bounded on the east by the Bloomingdale Road. It was called the Great Kills Farm after the stream which drained it. Another Hopper, Johannes, owned land farther north and had his house on the shore, near 52nd Street. This was reached from the Bloomingdale Road by Hopper Lane. When his sons married, Johannes built each a house, one at the junction of the Road and the Lane and the other nearby. The house shown in the sketch belonged to son, Andrew, and was still standing well into the 1860's.

Beekman is one of New York's oldest and most distinguished family names. The founder, William Beekman, came here from Holland on the ship with Peter Stuyvesant. He later became a burgomaster and acquired real estate. His name still survives in "William" and "Beekman" Streets. The family prospered and distinguished itself in various offices and, in 1763, James Beekman built a mansion at 51st Street near the East River. It was called Mount Pleasant and, between 1776 and 1783, due to its splendid location, was used as headquarters by the British commanders. In a greenhouse behind the mansion, the patriot Nathan Hale was imprisoned and tried. He was hanged in an orchard nearby, a sacrifice to his country. When the British Army left, on Evacuation Day, 1783, James Beekman returned to his home and entertained the American officers there. This famous old mansion survived until 1874.

Ever since the building of Fort Amsterdam, No. 1 Broadway has been a frame for a variety of pictures of Old New York. Among these pictures is the Kennedy Mansion. In 1745, Archibald Kennedy purchased the lots, Nos. 1, 2 and 3 Broadway, from Peter Bayard, a member of the Bayard family into which Peter Stuyvesant had married. In 1750, the palatial Kennedy Mansion was completed. Among its outstanding features were a grand staircase, a magnificent banquet hall and a parlor, fifty feet long, opening onto a spacious back porch which overlooked a garden running down to the Hudson's shore. Among these surroundings, Kennedy entertained the elite of the town. Came the Revolution; and Kennedy, a staunch Loyalist, left for England. General Israel Putnam now used the house as his headquarters. Then came Lord Cornwallis, Lord Howe and Sir Henry Clinton. Kennedy, in England, became the Earl of Cassilis and a member of the House of Lords.

BRIERLY

When the English took New York in 1664, having no building of their own, they held their religious services in "the church in the fort" after the Dutch had held their own services. This friendly arrangement lasted until 1692, when the real life of the Church of England began in the town. The Royal Instructions provided for the erection of churches and the appointment of clergymen by the Bishop of London. In 1698, the first church, Trinity, was built on Broadway at the head of Wall Street. As the population grew, this building became so crowded that it was necessary "to build a Chappel of Ease to Trinity Church", so several persons residing in "Montgomerie Ward" raised sufficient funds to buy land at Beekman and Cliff Streets and, in 1752, the second Protestant Episcopal Church, St. George's, was completed. Among its members were the Schuylers, Livingstons, Beekmans, Van Renselaers and Courtlandts. Washington Irving was christened here.

In 1770, the "Sign of the Dove" appeared on the old Post Road. Two years later, the stagecoach line to and from Boston would be traveling this road. The first vehicles, called "stage wagons" were boxlike affairs, accommodating eleven passengers and the driver. Passengers luckily occupying the rear seat, could lean against the high back of the wagon, but all other seats were without backs. Luggage was placed under the seats. These wagons had leather tops with side curtains as protection against bad weather. In summer the average speed was forty miles a day. In winter, top speed was twenty-five miles; so the lighted windows of a wayside inn, with its promised warmth and comfort, were a welcome sight to the frost-bitten, aching-backed traveler in the old stagecoach days.

This farmhouse, near the Hudson's shore, was, in 1773, the home of Jacob Harsen and his bride, Catherine Cozine Harsen. The Harsen family had come to lower New York in the preceding century. Jacob and Catherine were first cousins and, as infants, had slept in the same cradle when their mothers, Jannetje Dyckman Cozine and Rachel Harsen, had been visiting each other. This cradle of solid mahogany with brass handles was a family heirloom and occupied a prominent position in the old house. One night in 1805, a few neighbors met here and organized the Reformed Protestant Dutch Church of Harsenville. This hamlet, which had grown up around the Harsen farm, was in the Bloomingdale neighborhood and was named after Jacob Harsen's uncle (also named Jacob).

BRIERLY

William Alexander, erroneously called Lord Stirling, was the son of James Alexander, Colonial Secretary of New York. Upon his father's death in 1756, William inherited a large fortune. He joined the British Army and became aide-de-camp to Governor Shirley. In 1757, he went to London to lay claim to the Earldom of Stirling but was unsuccessful. After his return to New York and his marriage to Philip Livingston's daughter, he joined the Patriot cause and, in 1775, was a colonel in the Revolutionary Army. He first distinguished himself by capturing a British transport for which Congress made him a brigadier general. In addition to his military talents and personal bravery, he was a man of science with considerable knowledge of astronomy and mathematics. He was one of the founders of Columbia College.

PARK AVENUE AT THIRTY-SEVENTH STREET

This mansion stood on the "Middle Road", a short cut from the lower Post Road to the northern Kingsbridge section. It was owned by Robert Murray, a wealthy Quaker merchant, and was one of the loveliest spots on the island. Murray's wife, a former Philadelphia belle, was as clever as she was charming. Following the Battle of Long Island, General Putnam passed by in full retreat. Later, a far superior British force reached the house. Mrs. Murray, recognizing Lord Howe as their leader, suggested that he and his officers pause a moment for refreshment. It had been a long hot march, so Howe gladly acquiesced. He was so charmingly entertained that, by the time the march was resumed, "Old Put" and his men were safe at Harlem Heights. So Mrs. Murray made history. The Grand Central R. R. Station now covers Murray's cornfield.

From 1776 to 1783, the British occupied the city and the "Province Arms" had now become the "City Tavern". Under its new name, the old hostelry was as popular as ever, but now the scarlet coats of the army officers and the blue and gold of the navy added color to the scene. Good fellowship and conviviality reigned here, but there was also tragedy for, late one night, a duel was fought in one of the tavern's rooms. The principals in this affair of honor were the Honorable J. Tollemarche, brother of the Earl of Dysart and Commander of the man-of-war, Zebra, and Captain Pennington, of the Coldstream Guards. During the furious swordplay, Tollemarche received a thrust through the left breast and died instantly. His body was buried in Trinity Churchyard, but the exact location of the grave is unknown today.

In the spring of 1785, a carpenter's shop occupied the corner of Barclay and Church Streets. Acting for José Roiz Silva, an ardent Catholic, a certain Father Whelen procured a lease of this corner and, after fitting up the shop for divine services, started collecting funds for the erection of a church. Next, a letter signed by Silva and other leading church members was dispatched to Galway, Ireland, requesting contributions from Very Reverend Warden Augustine Kirwan. Then came the laying of the corner-stone, October 5th, 1785, by Don Diego de Gardoqui and in it were deposited Spanish coins. A generous contribution followed from the King of Spain and, on November 4th, 1786, the church was consecrated. For many years, every good Catholic able to walk or ride attended this historic house of worship, for it was New York's only Catholic Church until 1815. The present St. Peter's replaced it in 1836.

BRIERLY

Fraunces' Tavern, today, is one of the two Pre-Revolutionary buildings which have escaped destruction in lower New York. First, it was the residence of Stephen De Lancey from about 1720 until his death. After serving as a residence and a store, it was auctioned off to Samuel Fraunces. From 1762, it was operated as a tavern, first by Fraunces, then by Bolton (of Province Arms fame) and again by Fraunces, in 1770, when he refitted it and originated the additional service of delivering ready-cooked dinners to patrons living outside the tavern. At the close of the Revolution, Fraunces Tavern gained lasting fame as the scene of Washington's farewell to his comrades in arms. Later, when New York became the National Capital, Fraunces left the tavern to become President Washington's "Steward of the Household". He later accompanied the President to Philadelphia. The survival of this old landmark should be credited to the Society of the Sons of the Revolution.

BRIERLY

When New York was the National Capital in 1789, President Washington opened the Congress with pomp and formality, similar to the opening of Parliament by the King of England. Both houses of Congress were assembled in joint session and Washington delivered his message in person. After the address, he stepped into his waiting coach, drawn by six horses, and drove away, preceded by two mounted officers in full dress uniforms and followed by his secretary and two other gentlemen, these followed by his cabinet ministers in carriages. In those old days, high office was always associated with dignity and formality and Washington conducted himself in the punctilious manner which he felt his high position demanded. New Yorkers of Washington's time would, without doubt, have highly disapproved the broadly smiling, back-slapping and wise-cracking "statesmen" of the present.

CHERRY STREET

Cherry Street is one of New York's early thoroughfares. Where Pearl Street (called Queen Street after the British took over) ended at Peck Slip, a road continued in the same northerly direction into the open country. This road was bordered by farms and cherry orchards and was named Cherry Street. In 1770, Walter Franklin built a fine residence at No. 3. It was known as the Franklin House, and George Washington used it as a residence for about a year, following his inauguration as President in 1789. Until 1817, this location was known as St. George's Square, when it was re-named Franklin Square in honor of Benjamin Franklin. The mansion was destroyed in 1856. All that is left of it is a chair, made from some of the old timbers. The New York Historical Society has this chair. The abutment of Brooklyn Bridge covers the site of this old residence.

BRIERLY

In 1792, Cary Ludlow built this fine residence, at No. 9 State Street, then a residential section of the town. He was a member of a very distinguished family, who first came over here from England in 1694. (Their coat of arms appears in the sketch.) For about two centuries, the Ludlows formed an important element in the wealthy and influential population of the city. After Cary Ludlow's death in 1807, his widow continued to live in the mansion with her daughter, Catherine, and Catherine's husband, Jacob Morton. Susan Morton, a sister, was the wife of Josiah Quincy and her younger brother, Washington Morton, was the hero of a wild elopement with General Schuyler's daughter. Incidentally, General Schuyler's other daughter was the wife of Alexander Hamilton. The name "Ludlow" is conspicuous in Trinity Churchyard. It is also the name of a New York street.

BRIERLY

SPERO INFESTIS METUO SECUNDIS

LUDLOW ARMS

Following Washington's inauguration in 1789, it seemed apparent that New York City would continue to be the National Capital. Accordingly great plans were made to create a capital city that would arouse admiration throughout the world. It was proposed to cut off the lower end of Manhattan from river to river, at the foot of Broadway, and in this segregated district with its fine ocean setting, to erect magnificent parliamentary buildings, each surrounded by spacious grounds ornamented by shade trees and shrubbery. The first building was erected in 1790. It was called "Government House" and was to house the President, Senate and Representatives in separate wings and to accommodate visiting statesmen. When the National Capital was moved to Philadelphia this edifice became the residence of Governor Clinton and John Jay respectively. Later it became a custom house, 1799 to 1815.

BRIERLY

Richmond Hill once rose above a spot where today Varick and Charlton Streets merge. On top of this hill, and commanding a fine view of the Hudson, Abraham Mortier built a splendid residence in 1760. Later, Lord Amherst occupied it, after defeating the French in Canada. In 1776, Washington occupied it. Next came Howe and Cornwallis. Afterward, John Adams lived here while serving as Vice-President. In 1797, Aaron Burr took a long lease on the property, but after his unfortunate duel with Alexander Hamilton, he was forced to flee the country. As the city grew, this historic mansion, like most of its kind, went from bad to worse. The hill itself was cut down to the present street level and the old house was lowered with it. In 1831, it became a theatre, later a tavern and, in 1849, it was demolished to make way for modern houses.

BRIERLY

This cottage, facing the Bloomingdale Road, was built in 1716, not many years after the opening of this road. It stood in the midst of farm land first owned by the Horn family, on a spot just west of the present "Flatiron Building". The lovely stretch of country which started here and extended northward to 59th Street was called "Bloemen-dael" (vale of flowers) by the Dutch. When the "Commissioners' Plan" of streets was adopted, the old house was found to be standing right in the middle of the proposed Fifth Avenue so, in 1839, it was moved to the northwest corner of 23rd Street. It was later known as "Madison Cottage"; it was replaced by the famous Fifth Avenue Hotel. Today the Fifth Avenue Building occupies the site.

BROADWAY

In 1807, near the present Grace Church, Henry Brevoort kept a tavern. It was open country out here, but
New York was steadily growing and the "city fathers"
were planning new streets, intending to extend Broadway
northward in a straight line as far as 14th Street. This
would have made it necessary to chop down a very old
and beautiful tree, standing close to the tavern. Brevoort
had spent many happy hours smoking his pipe in the
shade of this old tree; so when he was informed of the
city planners' scheme, he lost no time in using all his
influence to change their plans. He was successful and,
instead of continuing Broadway in a straight line, they
"bent" it a little to the westward at 10th Street, thus
saving Henry's tree. Today, the tree, the tavern and the
tavern-keeper have all passed on, but the "bend" in
Broadway still survives.

BRIERLY

This beautiful church, St. John's, resembling St. Martin's in the Field, of London, was the architectural product of John McComb, Jr. It overlooked Hudson Square, later called St. John's Park, which, with its tall trees and shady walks, was one of New York's beauty spots. Throughout the day and evening, smart carriages drawn by spirited horses drew up before the stately mansions which surrounded the Park, and fashionably gowned ladies with their distinguished escorts promenaded along its gravel walks; for, following the erection of the church, St. John's Park had become one of the city's most fashionable residential districts. Sadly enough, the usual "progress" gradually transformed the mansions into boarding houses, tenements, and storage warehouses. The church, the last to go, was demolished in 1918 and, today, only memories and street names remain.

BRIERLY

EDGECOMBE AVENUE

Overlooking the Harlem River, this stately mansion has withstood the march of time since 1758. Roger Morris built it for his bride, Mary Philipse, a lady much admired by young George Washington. Years later, the same Washington (now General) used the mansion as his headquarters. In 1810, Stephen Jumel, a wealthy New York merchant, bought it. His wife, Madame (Eliza) Jumel started her romantic career by being born at sea in 1769; she was later adopted by a New England lady; next, as a beautiful, headstrong maiden of seventeen, she ran away to New York with a British army officer. Time passed and she became the bride of Jumel. She now presided at her husband's regally appointed mansion, dispensing hospitality to the elite. Later she continued her social success in Paris. Jumel died in 1832 and a year later she was won by Aaron Burr. They separated, however, in 1834. At the age of ninety-six, Madame finally passed away.

BRIERLY

New York's City Hall is one of our few buildings which has escaped demolition through the passing years. Mayor Edward Livingston and John McComb, the architect of the edifice, were present at the laying of the corner stone in 1803 but, due to the yellow fever epidemic, many prominent New Yorkers had left the city. Most of this city lay to the southward, so, although the front and sides of the building were to be of white marble, red sandstone was used on the back or Chambers Street side. When completed in 1812, the cost, exclusive of furnishings, was half a million dollars. The cupola which surmounted the structure was changed in 1830 to the present one. With this exception and with the removal of the high iron fence, which once surrounded the park, City Hall looks about as it did in 1812.

BRIERLY

In 1816, this tavern was well known and popular. It set well back from the east side of Broadway on rising ground, fully ten feet above the present street level. It had very little competition for, at this time, the city proper was south of a line drawn through Canal Street on the west, and Prince and Rivington Streets on the east. The city's population was over ninety-three thousand and Jacob Radcliffe was mayor. The City Hotel was the leading hostelry in town and Whitehall, Beaver, Broad and Pearl Streets as well as lower Broadway were where the "best people" had their residences. A few were able to maintain their own carriages, but most travelers used the stagecoach, which passed and often stopped at the Buck's Horn Tavern.

Here, Christian Bergh, a builder of square-rigged ships, could look out of his office window at a long line of shipyards, stretching along East River from Pike Street as far north as Eighth Street. Bergh was born in 1763 and rose to prominence as a shipbuilder during the War of 1812. His house was the rendezvous of many old shipbuilders and was noted for its huge fireplace. Before 1700, the name of Bergh was well-known in New York and his son, Henry, added renown to it by founding the Society for the Prevention of Cruelty to Animals. He had been in the diplomatic service in Europe and the merciless treatment of animals which he had seen there led to his militant interest in their protection, upon his return to America.

Here, on the corner of Nassau and Fulton Streets stood a tavern of solid yellow brick construction, built many years before the Revolution. After the War of 1812, it became famous as the Shakespeare Tavern, under the management of Thomas Hodgkinson, brother of John Hodgkinson of the Park Theatre. The tavern became a popular resort for actors, poets and literary men of the period and, on account of its famous clientele, was likened to the "Turk's Head" of London. In 1822, Hodgkinson built an extension on Fulton Street, with a large hall on the second floor, where public meetings and military drills were held. It was here that New York's famous Seventh Regiment was organized on August 25th, 1824.

Built on a ledge in the Hudson River a hundred yards off shore and called the Southwest Battery, this old pile was re-named Fort Clinton during the War of 1812. In 1822, it was discontinued as a fortification and ceded to the city. It now became a place of entertainment and in 1824 General Lafayette was officially welcomed here on his momentous visit to the United States. Other notables seen here were Henry Clay, Daniel Webster, President Jackson and Louis Kossuth. Here, also, P. T. Barnum staged Jennie Lind's first great triumph in 1850. Philip Hone gives a glowing description of Castle Garden as it then appeared and of the Italian Opera (tickets fifty cents). The building of the Academy of Music in 1854, ended Castle Garden's entertainment career. The space between the Garden and the mainland was filled in and the Board of Immigration took over from 1855 to 1890. After that it was transformed into the Municipal Aquarium. More recently it has been restored and declared a historic monument.

BRIERLY

In this fashionable section of the city, Philip Hone had his fine residence. He was a leader of society and entertained many of the visiting celebrities in his mansion. It was magnificently furnished with rare objects of art, which Hone had collected during his extensive travels abroad. About this time, he was appointed Mayor and served the city with distinction. He contributed generously to the original Mercantile Library Building and to many other benevolent and educational enterprises. Probably, without realizing it, his greatest contribution to posterity was a diary, which he had kept during his active life. This diary gives a fine and intimate picture of this interesting period of our national life.

James Monroe, fifth president of the United States and world famous for his "Monroe Doctrine", left his Virginia home, after his wife's death, and came to New York to live with his daughter and her husband, Samuel L. Gouverneur. Gouverneur, a former postmaster of the city, had a fine residence on the corner of Prince and Lafayette Streets and here the Ex-president eventually died, in 1831. After one of the most imposing funerals ever held in the city, his body was placed in a vault in the Marble Cemetery, but in 1858 it was removed to his native state of Virginia. Attempts were made to save the old house, built in 1823, as a national shrine, but unfortunately these attempts failed. The house was removed to No. 95 Crosby Street, where it followed the usual pattern of neglect and deterioration, and was finally destroyed.

BRIERLY

The name "Delmonico", of gastronomic fame, was first seen at No. 23 William Street in 1829. The Delmonico Brothers, newly arrived from Italy, started business with a few small tables and a long counter, behind which one of the brothers, with a white cap and perfect manners, served dainty cakes and specialties and sold delicious confections. These Italians had been trained in Europe and their excellent food and attentive service were in such contrast to that which the first few customers had received at the nearby boarding houses, that it started gossip and soon more customers appeared. The result was a steady growth of business, larger and better quarters and eventually, a group of the finest restaurants that New York had ever seen, serving a most discriminating clientele. Before Delmonico's, dining in New York was, to a great extent, a crude function merely to satisfy hunger. After Delmonico's, it became a fine art.

Samuel Ward, famous in New York banking circles, was founder and first president of the Bank of Commerce. His house, on the corner of Bond Street, was noted for its private picture gallery, the first in America. Ward had three daughters and one of them, Julia, born in 1819, was much admired by Dr. Samuel Gridley Howe, who had served as Surgeon General in the Greek Army with Lord Byron. The friendship of this cultured and philanthropic gentleman with the carefully educated and talented young lady resulted in marriage. With her husband, Julia Ward Howe engaged in many worth-while activities during her long life. Perhaps she is best remembered for her *Battle Hymn of the Republic,* written while visiting an army camp.

NINTH AVENUE AND TWENTY-THIRD STREET

This mansion was built by Mistress Molly Clarke about 1750. In 1802, she bequeathed it to her son-in-law, Bishop Benjamin Moore, and he willed it to his son, Clement C. Moore, in 1812. Clement studied for the ministry at Columbia but never took orders; instead, he devoted himself to the development and improvement of Chelsea Village, resulting in the creation of old London Terrace and Chelsea Cottages. He gave, rent free, an entire city block (Chelsea Square) to the General Theological Seminary of the Protestant Episcopal Church, of which he was a faculty member until his death in 1863. Today the mansion and the Doctor have passed away but his poem, "A Visit from St. Nicholas", written in a period of relaxation, will keep green the memory of Clement C. Moore for many a Christmas yet to come. " 'Twas the night before Christmas and all through the house, not a creature was stirring, not even a mouse."

Harvard and Yale in New England may have created a desire among New Yorkers to have a college. The result of this desire was King's College, founded in 1754. The money required for its founding was raised by the Provincial Assembly, through a public lottery; the land upon which to build it (a plot bounded by Church, Murray and Barclay Streets) was a gift from Trinity Church. The grounds ran across the present Park Place, which was then called Robinson Street, and ended at Church Street. In 1784, after the Revolution, the college was re-named Columbia and more buildings were added from time to time, until 1857, when it moved to a new location between 49th and 50th Streets and Madison and Fourth Avenues, where it remained until 1897. As Columbia University, it now stands on Morningside Heights, *nulli secundus*.

On the south side of Bleecker Street, around 1850, between Thompson and Sullivan Streets (numbers 158-60-62-64), there was a "row of elegant buildings" known as Depau Row. They were erected in the late 1840's by Francis Depau, a cultured French gentleman, as a venture in real estate. Depau, having accumulated a fortune by shipping cotton to Europe from South Carolina and, in New York, having established the Havre Line of Packets, was a member of the city's best society and Depau Row became a fashionable neighborhood at about the time when St. John's Park was still popular. The present day Bleecker Street, dingy and dilapidated, bears little resemblance to the distinguished Depau Row of long ago.

In 1844, the U. S. Government took a seven-year lease of this old edifice and transformed it into a Post Office. It was considered to be an "immense establishment" and employed seventy-six clerks. This was before adhesive stamps were used and, on each letter, the postmaster or a clerk stamped or wrote the word "Paid". For greater convenience, in 1845, the Postmaster of New York, Robert H. Morris, issued an adhesive of his own, the first of the rare "Postmaster's Provisionals". In 1847, the Government followed with the first general issue of adhesive stamps. Originally, this building was the Middle Dutch Church and, in 1728, a member of the De Peyster family bequeathed to it a bell which, at the age of two hundred and twenty-five years, now reposes in the present Middle Dutch Church on Second Avenue.

POST OFFICE

BRIERLY

In 1855, the horsecar shown here, ran through Canal and Hudson Streets and Eighth Avenue to Central Park. It was a great improvement upon its predecessors. Inside, at the front end, there was a fare-box, where the passengers dropped their money. Upon reaching the northern end of the line, the body of the car could be swung around on the wheelbase and, after hitching up the horses again, the driver climbed up to his old seat, now facing south, and was ready for the return trip. The original horsecar on the Fourth Avenue Line in 1832, said to be the first horsecar line in the world, looked very much like a double stagecoach, with a high seat at each end. By 1867, there were eight hundred horsecars in the city.

On March 20th, 1804, a group of prominent citizens met
"to collect and preserve whatever may relate to the natural,
civil and ecclesiastical history of the United States in general and this city in particular." From this meeting the
New York Historical Society evolved. The society first
met in the old City Hall at Wall Street and Nassau, and
at various other places until 1857, when it erected its own
building. From this location, the society moved uptown to
its present quarters at Central Park West. Here, amid
charming surroundings, one can study at close range the
finest examples of the actual furniture, china, utensils
and costumes which our forefathers used and wore, besides old vehicles, ship models, paintings, prints and books
of historic interest.

BRIERLY

This little house was built in 1810 and, in 1846, Edgar Allan Poe lived here with his young wife, Virginia, and her mother. It is said that Poe often walked across the fields to the Harlem River, nearby, jumped into a boat and rowed all the way down to lower Manhattan, to the office of the Broadway Journal. In this cottage, he wrote *Annabel Lee* and, a short time previously, *The Raven*. Here, also, he received one of his saddest blows, when his young wife passed away, early in 1847, after a wasting illness. Poe never really recovered from this misfortune. His health failed, his writings became less frequent and, in 1849, death ended his career. Only four persons, besides the officiating clergyman, attended the funeral of this unfortunate man, whose fame is now worldwide.